Table of Contents

Waikiki Cookies

1½ **cups packed light brown sugar**
⅔ **cup shortening**
1 **tablespoon water**
1 **teaspoon vanilla**
2 **eggs**
1¾ **cups all-purpose flour**
½ **teaspoon salt**
¼ **teaspoon baking soda**
1 **cup white chocolate chunks**
1 **cup macadamia nuts, coarsely chopped**

1. Preheat oven to 375°F.

2. Combine brown sugar, shortening, water and vanilla in large bowl. Beat with electric mixer at medium speed until well blended. Add eggs; beat well.

3. Combine flour, salt and baking soda in medium bowl. Add to sugar mixture; beat at low speed just until blended. Stir in white chocolate chunks and nuts.

4. Drop dough by rounded tablespoonfuls 2 inches apart onto ungreased baking sheets.

5. Bake 7 to 9 minutes or until cookies are set. Do not overbake. Cool 2 minutes on baking sheets. Remove cookies to wire racks; cool completely.

Makes about 3 dozen cookies

Black & White Hearts

1 cup (2 sticks) butter, softened
¾ cup sugar
1 package (3 ounces) cream cheese, softened
1 egg
1½ teaspoons vanilla
3 cups all-purpose flour
1 cup semisweet chocolate chips
2 tablespoons shortening

1. Combine butter, sugar, cream cheese, egg and vanilla in large bowl. Beat with electric mixer at medium speed, scraping bowl often, until light and fluffy. Add flour; beat until well blended. Divide dough in half; wrap each half in waxed paper. Refrigerate 2 hours or until firm.

2. Preheat oven to 375°F. Roll dough to ⅛-inch thickness on lightly floured surface. Cut dough with lightly floured 2-inch heart-shaped cookie cutter. Place cutouts 1 inch apart on ungreased cookie sheets. Bake 7 to 10 minutes or until edges are very lightly browned. Remove immediately to wire racks to cool completely.

3. Melt chocolate chips and shortening in small saucepan over low heat 4 to 6 minutes or until melted. Dip half of each heart into melted chocolate. Refrigerate on cookie sheets or trays lined with waxed paper until chocolate is set. Store, covered, in refrigerator. *Makes about 3½ dozen cookies*

Rum Fruitcake Cookies

1 cup sugar
¾ cup shortening
3 eggs
⅓ cup orange juice
1 tablespoon rum extract
3 cups all-purpose flour
2 teaspoons baking powder
1 teaspoon baking soda
1 teaspoon salt
2 cups (8 ounces) chopped candied mixed fruit
1 cup raisins
1 cup nuts, coarsely chopped

1. Preheat oven to 375°F. Lightly grease cookie sheets; set aside. Beat sugar and shortening in large bowl until fluffy. Add eggs, orange juice and rum extract; beat 2 minutes.

2. Combine flour, baking powder, baking soda and salt in medium bowl. Add candied fruit, raisins and nuts. Stir into creamed mixture. Drop dough by rounded teaspoonfuls 2 inches apart onto prepared cookie sheets. Bake 10 to 12 minutes or until golden. Let cookies stand on cookie sheets 2 minutes. Remove to wire racks; cool completely. *Makes about 6 dozen cookies*

Pebbernødders

3 cups all-purpose flour
1 teaspoon baking powder
1 teaspoon cinnamon
$\frac{1}{2}$ teaspoon ginger
$\frac{1}{2}$ teaspoon ground cloves
$1\frac{1}{2}$ cups (3 sticks) butter
$1\frac{1}{2}$ cups sugar
3 eggs
2 teaspoons grated lemon peel

1. Grease cookie sheets. Combine flour, baking powder, cinnamon, ginger and cloves; set aside. Beat butter and sugar in large bowl with electric mixer at medium speed until creamy. Add eggs and lemon peel; mix well. Gradually add flour mixture to butter mixture; mix just until well blended. Refrigerate dough 2 hours or until firm.

2. Roll dough into 12-inch long ropes about $\frac{3}{4}$ inch thick. Freeze rolls on cookie sheets until hard.

3. Preheat oven to 375°F. Slice frozen rolls $\frac{1}{8}$ inch thick. Arrange 1 inch apart on prepared cookie sheets. Bake 10 minutes or until lightly browned.

Makes about 66 dozen $\frac{3}{4}$-inch cookies

Chocolate–Dipped Biscotti Nuggets

¾ **cup uncooked old-fashioned or quick oats**
2¼ **cups all-purpose flour**
1½ **teaspoons baking powder**
½ **teaspoon salt**
¾ **cup chopped dates**
½ **cup coarsely chopped toasted pecans**
½ **cup honey**
2 **eggs**
1 **teaspoon vanilla**
½ **cup (1 stick) butter, melted**
Grated peel of 2 oranges
1¾ **cups semisweet chocolate chips or white chocolate chips**
4 **teaspoons shortening**

1. Grease baking sheet; set aside. Preheat oven to 350°F. Place oats in food processor; process until oats resemble coarse flour. Combine oats, flour, baking powder and salt in large bowl. Stir in dates and pecans.

2. Whisk together honey, eggs and vanilla in medium bowl. Add melted butter and orange peel. Stir egg mixture into oat mixture just until blended. Turn out dough onto lightly floured surface; flatten slightly. Knead until dough holds together, adding flour if necessary to prevent sticking. Divide dough into 3 equal pieces; shape each into 9×2-inch log. Carefully transfer logs to prepared baking sheet, spacing about 2 inches apart. If dough cracks, pat back into shape.

3. Bake logs 25 to 30 minutes or until lightly golden but still soft. Remove from oven. *Reduce oven temperature to 275°F.* Let logs cool on baking sheet 10 minutes. Trim ends using serrated knife. Slice logs on slight diagonal, about ¾ inch thick. Arrange biscotti on their sides on baking sheet. Return to oven and bake 15 to 20 minutes or until lightly golden. Turn biscotti over and bake 10 to 15 minutes longer. Remove biscotti to wire rack to cool completely.

4. Brush individual biscotti with dry pastry brush to remove any loose crumbs. Heat chocolate chips and shortening in small heavy saucepan over very low heat until melted and smooth. Dip half of each biscotti slice into melted chocolate, letting any excess run off. Place on waxed paper. Let stand until set. Store in waxed paper-lined container at room temperature.

Makes about 36 cookies

Double Chocolate Cranberry Chunkies

1¾ **cups all-purpose flour**
⅓ **cup unsweetened cocoa powder**
½ **teaspoon baking powder**
½ **teaspoon salt**
1 **cup butter, softened**
1 **cup granulated sugar**
½ **cup packed brown sugar**
1 **egg**
1 **teaspoon vanilla**
2 **cups semisweet chocolate chunks or large chocolate chips**
¾ **cup dried cranberries or dried tart cherries**
  Additional granulated sugar

1. Preheat oven to 350°F.

2. Combine flour, cocoa, baking powder and salt in small bowl; set aside. Beat butter, 1 cup granulated sugar and brown sugar in large bowl with electric mixer at medium speed until light and fluffy. Beat in egg and vanilla until well blended. Gradually beat in flour mixture at low speed until blended. Stir in chocolate chunks and cranberries.

3. Drop dough by level ¼ cupfuls onto ungreased cookie sheets, spacing 3 inches apart. Flatten dough until 2 inches in diameter with bottom of glass that has been dipped in additional granulated sugar.

4. Bake 11 to 12 minutes or until cookies are set. Cool cookies 2 minutes on cookie sheets; transfer to wire racks. Cool completely.

Makes about 1 dozen (4-inch) cookies

Double Lemon Delights

2¼ **cups all-purpose flour**
½ **teaspoon baking powder**
½ **teaspoon salt**
1 **cup (2 sticks) butter, softened**
¾ **cup granulated sugar**
1 **egg**
2 **tablespoons grated lemon peel, divided**
1 **teaspoon vanilla**
   Additional granulated sugar
1 **cup powdered sugar**
4 **to 5 teaspoons lemon juice**

1. Preheat oven to 375°F.

2. Combine flour, baking powder and salt in small bowl; set aside. Beat butter and granulated sugar in large bowl with electric mixer at medium speed until light and fluffy. Beat in egg, 1 tablespoon lemon peel and vanilla until well blended. Gradually beat in flour mixture at low speed until blended.

3. Drop dough by level ¼ cupfuls onto ungreased cookie sheets, spacing 3 inches apart. Flatten dough until 3 inches in diameter with bottom of glass that has been dipped in additional granulated sugar.

4. Bake 12 to 14 minutes or until cookies are just set and edges are golden brown. Cool on cookie sheets 2 minutes; transfer to wire racks. Cool completely.

5. Combine powdered sugar, lemon juice and remaining 1 tablespoon lemon peel in small bowl; drizzle over cookies. Let stand until icing is set.

Makes about 1 dozen (4-inch) cookies

Variation: To make smaller cookies, drop 2 tablespoons dough 2 inches apart onto ungreased cookie sheets. Bake 8 to 10 minutes or until cookies are just set and edges are golden brown. Cool on cookie sheets 2 minutes; transfer to wire racks. Cool completely. Continue with Step 5. Makes about 2 dozen cookies.

Smilin' Cookies

1 package (18 ounces) refrigerated sugar cookie dough
1 tablespoon plus 1 teaspoon finely grated lemon peel
Yellow food coloring and yellow crystal sugar
¼ cup semisweet or milk chocolate chips

1. Remove dough from wrapper; place in large bowl. Let dough stand at room temperature about 15 minutes.

2. Add lemon peel and food coloring to dough; beat with electric mixer at medium speed until well blended and evenly colored. Wrap dough in plastic wrap; freeze 30 minutes.

3. Preheat oven to 350°F. Shape dough into 32 balls. Place 2 inches apart on ungreased cookie sheets; flatten into 1¾-inch rounds. Sprinkle with yellow sugar.

4. Bake 9 to 11 minutes or until set. Cool on cookie sheets 2 minutes. Remove to wire racks; cool completely.

5. Place chocolate chips in small resealable plastic food storage bag; seal. Microwave at HIGH (100% power) 1 minute; knead bag lightly. Microwave at HIGH for additional 30-second intervals until chips are completely melted, kneading bag after each interval. Cut off very tiny corner of bag. Pipe chocolate onto cookies for eyes and mouths. *Makes 32 cookies*

Peanuts

½ cup (1 stick) butter, softened
¼ cup shortening
¼ cup creamy peanut butter
1 cup powdered sugar, sifted
1 egg yolk
1 teaspoon vanilla
1¾ cups all-purpose flour
1 cup finely ground honey-roasted peanuts, divided
Peanut Buttery Frosting (recipe follows)

1. Beat butter, shortening and peanut butter in large bowl with electric mixer at medium speed. Gradually add powdered sugar, beating until smooth. Add egg yolk and vanilla; beat well. Add flour; mix well. Stir in ⅓ cup ground peanuts. Cover dough; refrigerate 1 hour. Prepare Peanut Buttery Frosting.

2. Preheat oven to 350°F. Grease cookie sheets. Shape dough into 1-inch balls. Place 2 balls, side by side and slightly touching, on prepared cookie sheet. Gently flatten balls with fingertips to form into "peanut" shape. Repeat steps with remaining dough.

3. Bake 16 to 18 minutes or until edges are lightly browned. Cool on cookie sheets 5 minutes. Remove cookies to wire racks; cool completely.

4. Place remaining ⅔ cup ground peanuts in shallow dish. Spread about 2 teaspoons Peanut Buttery Frosting evenly over top of each cookie. Coat with ground peanuts.

Makes about 2 dozen cookies

Peanut Buttery Frosting

½ cup (1 stick) butter or margarine, softened
½ cup creamy peanut butter
2 cups powdered sugar, sifted
½ teaspoon vanilla
3 to 6 tablespoons milk

1. Beat butter and peanut butter in medium bowl with electric mixer at medium speed until smooth. Gradually add powdered sugar and vanilla until blended but crumbly.

2. Add milk 1 tablespoon at a time until smooth. Refrigerate until ready to use.

Makes 1⅓ cups frosting

Twisty Sticks

1 package (18 ounces) refrigerated sugar cookie dough
6 tablespoons all-purpose flour, divided
1 tablespoon unsweetened cocoa powder
2 tablespoons creamy peanut butter
1 cup semisweet chocolate chips
1 tablespoon shortening
   Colored sprinkles and finely chopped peanuts

1. Remove dough from wrapper. Divide dough in half; place in separate medium bowls. Let dough stand at room temperature about 15 minutes.

2. Add 3 tablespoons flour and cocoa powder to one dough half; beat at medium speed of electric mixer until well blended. Wrap in plastic wrap; refrigerate at least 1 hour.

3. Add remaining 3 tablespoons flour and peanut butter to other dough half; beat at medium speed of electric mixer until well blended. Wrap in plastic wrap; refrigerate at least 1 hour.

4. Preheat oven to 350°F. Divide chocolate dough into 30 equal pieces. Divide peanut butter dough into 30 equal pieces. Shape each dough piece into 4-inch-long rope on lightly floured surface. For each cookie, twist 1 chocolate rope and 1 peanut butter rope together. Place 2 inches apart on ungreased cookie sheets. Bake 7 to 10 minutes or until set. Remove to wire rack; cool completely.

5. Combine chocolate chips and shortening in small microwavable bowl. Microwave at HIGH (100% power) 1 minute; stir. Microwave at HIGH for additional 30-second intervals until chips and shortening are completely melted and smooth. Spread chocolate on 1 end of each cookie; top with sprinkles and peanuts as desired. Place on waxed paper. Let stand 30 minutes or until set. *Makes 2½ dozen cookies*

Peanut Butter Chocolate Chippers

1 cup packed light brown sugar
1 cup creamy or chunky peanut butter
1 large egg
¾ cup milk chocolate chips
Granulated sugar

1. Preheat oven to 350°F.

2. Combine brown sugar, peanut butter and egg in medium bowl; mix until well blended. Add chips; mix well.

3. Shape heaping tablespoonfuls of dough into 1½-inch balls. Place balls 2 inches apart on ungreased cookie sheets.

4. Dip table fork into granulated sugar; press criss-cross fashion onto each ball, flattening to ½-inch thickness.

5. Bake 12 minutes or until set. Let cookies stand on cookie sheets 2 minutes. Remove cookies with spatula to wire racks; cool completely.

Makes about 2 dozen cookies

Note: This simple recipe is unusual because it doesn't contain any flour—but it still makes great cookies!

Cocoa Hazelnut Macaroons

⅓ cup hazelnuts
¾ cup quick oats
⅓ cup light brown sugar
6 tablespoons unsweetened cocoa powder
2 tablespoons all-purpose flour
4 egg whites
1 teaspoon vanilla
½ teaspoon salt
⅓ cup plus 1 tablespoon granulated sugar

1. Preheat oven to 375°F. Spread hazelnuts in even layer on cookie sheet. Bake 8 minutes or until lightly browned. Quickly transfer nuts to clean dry dish towel. Fold towel; rub vigorously to remove as much of the skins as possible. Finely chop nuts using food processor or chef's knife. Combine with oats, brown sugar, cocoa and flour in medium bowl; mix well. Set aside.

2. Reduce oven temperature to 325°F. Combine egg whites, vanilla and salt in clean, dry medium mixing bowl. Beat with electric mixer at high speed until soft peaks form. Gradually add granulated sugar; continue to beat on high until stiff peaks form. Gently fold in hazelnut mixture with rubber spatula.

3. Drop level tablespoonfuls of dough onto cookie sheet. Bake 15 to 17 minutes or until tops of cookies no longer appear wet. Transfer to cooling rack. Store in loosely covered container. *Makes 3 dozen cookies*

Tie-Dyed T-Shirts

1 package (18 ounces) refrigerated sugar cookie dough
6 tablespoons all-purpose flour, divided
Red, yellow and blue food colorings

1. Preheat oven to 350°F. Grease cookie sheets.

2. Remove dough from wrapper. Divide into 3 pieces; place in separate medium bowls. Let stand at room temperature about 15 minutes.

3. Add 2 tablespoons flour and red food coloring to dough in one bowl; beat at medium speed of electric mixer until well blended and evenly colored. Wrap in plastic wrap; refrigerate 20 minutes. Repeat with second dough piece, 2 tablespoons flour and yellow food coloring. Repeat with remaining dough piece, remaining 2 tablespoons flour and blue food coloring.

4. Divide each color in half. Press together half of yellow dough with half of red dough. Roll dough on lightly floured surface to $1/4$-inch thickness. Cut dough with 3-inch T-shirt-shaped cookie cutter. Place cutouts 2 inches apart on prepared cookie sheets. Repeat with remaining dough, pairing remaining yellow dough with half of blue dough and remaining red dough with remaining blue dough.

5. Bake 7 to 9 minutes or until firm but not browned. Cool completely on cookie sheets.

Makes about 1½ dozen cookies

Cinnamon Swirls

1 package (18 ounces) refrigerated sugar cookie dough
½ **cup packed light brown sugar**
2 teaspoons ground cinnamon
1 cup powdered sugar
2 to 3 tablespoons milk
½ **cup finely chopped walnuts or pecans (optional)**

1. Remove dough from wrapper; divide dough in half. Wrap 1 dough half in plastic wrap; refrigerate. Place remaining dough half in medium bowl; let stand at room temperature about 15 minutes.

2. Add brown sugar and cinnamon to dough in bowl; beat with electric mixer at medium speed until well blended. Wrap dough in plastic wrap; refrigerate until needed.

3. Roll plain dough on lightly floured surface to form 8-inch square. Repeat with cinnamon dough; place cinnamon dough on top of plain dough. Roll up doughs into 10-inch log. Wrap log in plastic wrap; freeze at least 1 hour before slicing.

4. Preheat oven to 350°F. Grease cookie sheets. Cut dough log into ³/₈-inch slices; place on prepared cookie sheets. Bake 10 to 12 minutes or until cookies are lightly browned. Remove to wire racks; cool completely.

5. For icing, mix powdered sugar and 2 tablespoons milk in small bowl until smooth; add additional milk to reach drizzling consistency if necessary. Drizzle icing over cooled cookies; sprinkle with nuts, if desired.

Makes 2 dozen cookies

Chocolate and Peanut Butter Hearts

Chocolate Cookie Dough (recipe follows)
1 **cup sugar**
$\frac{1}{2}$ **cup creamy peanut butter**
$\frac{1}{2}$ **cup shortening**
1 **egg**
3 **tablespoons milk**
1 **teaspoon vanilla**
2 **cups all-purpose flour**
1 **teaspoon baking powder**
$\frac{1}{4}$ **teaspoon salt**

1. Prepare and chill Chocolate Cookie Dough as directed.

2. Beat sugar, peanut butter and shortening until fluffy. Add egg, milk and vanilla; mix well. Combine flour, baking powder and salt. Beat flour mixture into peanut butter mixture until well blended. Shape dough into disc. Wrap in plastic wrap; refrigerate 1 to 2 hours or until firm.

3. Preheat oven to 350°F. Grease cookie sheets. Roll peanut butter dough on floured waxed paper to $\frac{1}{8}$-inch thickness. Cut dough using 3-inch heart-shaped cookie cutter. Place cutouts on prepared cookie sheets. Repeat with chocolate dough.

4. Use smaller heart-shaped cookie cutter to remove small section from centers of hearts. Place small peanut butter hearts into large chocolate hearts; place small chocolate hearts into large peanut butter hearts. Press together lightly.

5. Bake 12 to 14 minutes or until edges are lightly browned. Remove to wire racks; cool completely. *Makes 4 dozen cookies*

Chocolate Cookie Dough

1 **cup (2 sticks) butter, softened**
1 **cup sugar**
1 **egg**
1 **teaspoon vanilla**
2 **ounces semisweet chocolate, melted**
$2\frac{1}{4}$ **cups all-purpose flour**
1 **teaspoon baking powder**
$\frac{1}{4}$ **teaspoon salt**

1. Beat butter and sugar in large bowl at high speed of electric mixer until fluffy. Beat in egg and vanilla. Add melted chocolate; mix well.

2. Add flour, baking powder and salt; mix well. Cover; refrigerate about 2 hours or until firm.

Mocha Crinkles

1⅓ **cups packed light brown sugar**
½ **cup vegetable oil**
¼ **cup reduced-fat sour cream**
1 **egg**
1 **teaspoon vanilla**
1¾ **cups all-purpose flour**
¾ **cup unsweetened cocoa powder**
2 **teaspoons instant espresso or coffee granules**
1 **teaspoon baking soda**
¼ **teaspoon salt**
⅛ **teaspoon black pepper**
½ **cup powdered sugar**

1. Beat brown sugar and oil in medium bowl with electric mixer at medium speed. Mix in sour cream, egg and vanilla; set aside.

2. Mix flour, cocoa, espresso, baking soda, salt and pepper in another medium bowl. Add flour mixture to brown sugar mixture; mix well. Refrigerate dough until firm, 3 to 4 hours.

3. Preheat oven to 350°F. Pour powdered sugar into shallow bowl. Set aside. Roll dough into 1-inch balls. Roll balls in powdered sugar.

4. Bake on ungreased cookie sheets 10 to 12 minutes or until tops of cookies are firm to touch. *(Do not overbake.)* Cool on wire racks.

Makes about 6 dozen cookies

Date Pinwheel Cookies

1¼ **cups dates, pitted and finely chopped**
¾ **cup orange juice**
½ **cup granulated sugar**
1 **tablespoon butter**
3 **cups plus 1 tablespoon all-purpose flour, divided**
2 **teaspoons vanilla, divided**
1 **cup packed brown sugar**
4 **ounces cream cheese**
¼ **cup shortening**
2 **eggs**
1 **teaspoon baking soda**
½ **teaspoon salt**

1. Heat dates, orange juice, granulated sugar, butter and 1 tablespoon flour in medium saucepan over medium heat. Cook 10 minutes or until thick, stirring frequently; remove from heat. Stir in 1 teaspoon vanilla; set aside to cool.

2. Beat brown sugar, cream cheese and shortening about 3 minutes in large bowl with electric mixer until light and fluffy. Add eggs and remaining 1 teaspoon vanilla; beat 2 minutes longer.

3. Combine remaining 3 cups flour, baking soda and salt in medium bowl. Add to shortening mixture; stir just until blended. Divide dough in half. Roll one half of dough on lightly floured surface into 12×9-inch rectangle. Spread half of date mixture over dough. Spread evenly, leaving ¼-inch border at top short edge. Starting at short side, tightly roll up dough jelly-roll style. Wrap in plastic wrap; freeze at least 1 hour. Repeat with remaining dough and date mixture.

4. Preheat oven to 350°F. Grease cookie sheets. Unwrap dough. Using heavy thread or dental floss, cut dough into ¼-inch slices. Place slices 1 inch apart on prepared cookie sheets.

5. Bake 12 minutes or until lightly browned. Let cookies stand on cookie sheets 2 minutes. Remove cookies to wire racks; cool completely.

Makes 6 dozen cookies

Ultimate Chippers

2½ cups all-purpose flour
1 teaspoon baking soda
½ teaspoon salt
1 cup (2 sticks) butter, softened
1 cup packed light brown sugar
½ cup granulated sugar
2 eggs
1 tablespoon vanilla
1 cup semisweet chocolate chips
1 cup milk chocolate chips
1 cup white chocolate chips
½ cup coarsely chopped pecans (optional)

Preheat oven to 375°F. Combine flour, baking soda and salt in medium bowl.

Beat butter, brown sugar and granulated sugar in large bowl until light and fluffy. Beat in eggs and vanilla. Add flour mixture to butter mixture; beat until well blended. Stir in chips and pecans, if desired.

Drop dough by heaping teaspoonfuls 2 inches apart onto ungreased cookie sheets. Bake 10 to 12 minutes or until edges are golden brown. Let cookies stand on cookie sheets 2 minutes. Remove cookies to wire racks; cool completely.   *Makes about 6 dozen cookies*

Swedish Cookie Shells

1 cup (2 sticks) butter, softened
$^2/_3$ cup sugar
1 large egg white
1 teaspoon vanilla
$^1/_2$ teaspoon almond extract
2 cups all-purpose flour, divided
$^1/_4$ cup finely ground blanched almonds

1. Beat butter and sugar in large bowl until light and fluffy. Beat in egg white, vanilla and almond extract until well blended. Gradually add $1^1/_2$ cups flour and almonds. Beat until well blended. Stir in enough remaining flour with spoon to form soft dough. Form dough into 1-inch-thick square; wrap in plastic wrap and refrigerate until firm, 1 hour or overnight.

2. Preheat oven to 375°F. Press rounded teaspoonfuls of dough into greased sandbakelser tins* or mini muffin pan cups. Place tins on baking sheet. Bake 8 to 10 minutes or until cookie shells are lightly browned. Cool cookies in tins 1 minute.

3. Carefully loosen cookies from tins with point of small knife. Invert tins over wire racks and tap lightly to release cookies; cool completely (cookies should be shell-side up). Repeat with remaining dough; cool cookie tins between batches.

4. Serve cookies shell-side up. Store tightly covered at room temperature or freeze up to 3 months. *Makes about 10 dozen cookies*

Sandbakelser tins are little tart pans (2 to 3 inches in diameter) with fluted edges.

Buttery Almond Cutouts

1½ **cups granulated sugar**
1 **cup (2 sticks) butter, softened**
¾ **cup sour cream**
2 **eggs**
3 **teaspoons almond extract, divided**
1 **teaspoon vanilla**
4⅓ **cups all-purpose flour**
1 **teaspoon baking powder**
1 **teaspoon baking soda**
½ **teaspoon salt**
2 **cups powdered sugar**
2 **tablespoons milk**
1 **tablespoon light corn syrup**
   Assorted food colorings

1. Beat granulated sugar and butter in large bowl until light and fluffy. Add sour cream, eggs, 2 teaspoons almond extract and vanilla; beat until smooth. Add flour, baking powder, baking soda and salt; beat just until well blended.

2. Divide dough into 4 pieces; flatten each piece into disc. Wrap each disc tightly with plastic wrap. Refrigerate at least 3 hours or up to 3 days.

3. Combine powdered sugar, milk, corn syrup and remaining 1 teaspoon almond extract in small bowl; stir until smooth. Cover and refrigerate up to 3 days.

4. Preheat oven to 375°F. Working with 1 disc of dough at a time, roll out on floured surface to ¼-inch thickness. Cut dough into desired shapes using 2½-inch cookie cutters. Place about 2 inches apart on ungreased baking sheets. Bake 7 to 8 minutes or until edges are firm and bottoms are brown. Remove from baking sheets to wire racks to cool.

5. Separate powdered sugar mixture into 3 or 4 batches in small bowls; tint each batch with desired food coloring. Frost cookies.

Makes about 3 dozen cookies

Note: To freeze dough, place wrapped discs in resealable plastic food storage bags. Thaw at room temperature before using. Or, cut out dough, bake and cool cookies completely. Freeze unglazed cookies for up to 2 months. Thaw and glaze as desired.

Banana Chocolate Chip Softies

1¼ cups all-purpose flour
1 teaspoon baking powder
½ teaspoon salt
⅓ cup butter, softened
⅓ cup granulated sugar
⅓ cup packed light brown sugar
1 ripe medium banana, mashed
1 egg
1 teaspoon vanilla
1 cup milk chocolate chips
½ cup coarsely chopped walnuts (optional)

1. Preheat oven to 375°F. Lightly grease cookie sheets.

2. Place flour, baking powder and salt in small bowl; stir.

3. Beat butter and sugars in large bowl with electric mixer at medium speed until light and fluffy. Beat in banana, egg and vanilla. Add flour mixture. Beat at low speed until well blended. Stir in chocolate chips and walnuts, if desired. (Dough will be soft.)

4. Drop rounded teaspoonfuls of dough 2 inches apart onto prepared cookie sheets.

5. Bake 9 to 11 minutes or until edges are golden brown. Let cookies stand on cookie sheets 2 minutes. Remove cookies to wire racks; cool completely. Store tightly covered at room temperature. *Makes about 3 dozen cookies*

Note: These cookies do not freeze well.

Oatmeal Candied Chippers

¾ cup (1½ sticks) butter, softened
¾ cup granulated sugar
¾ cup packed light brown sugar
3 tablespoons milk
1 egg
2 teaspoons vanilla
¾ cup all-purpose flour
¾ teaspoon salt
½ teaspoon baking soda
3 cups uncooked old-fashioned or quick oats
1⅓ cups (10-ounce package) candy-coated semisweet chocolate chips or candy-coated chocolate pieces

Preheat oven to 375°F. Grease cookie sheets; set aside. Beat butter, granulated sugar and brown sugar in large bowl until light and fluffy. Add milk, egg and vanilla; beat well. Add flour, salt and baking soda. Beat until well blended. Stir in oats and chocolate chips.

Drop by rounded tablespoonfuls 2 inches apart onto prepared cookie sheets. Bake 10 to 12 minutes or until edges are golden brown. Let cookies stand 2 minutes on cookie sheets. Remove cookies to wire racks; cool completely.

Makes about 4 dozen cookies

Canned Peanut Butter Candy Cookies

¾ **cup chunky peanut butter**
½ **cup (1 stick) butter, softened**
 1 **cup packed light brown sugar**
½ **teaspoon baking powder**
½ **teaspoon baking soda**
 1 **egg**
1½ **teaspoons vanilla**
1¼ **cups all-purpose flour**
 2 **cups quartered miniature peanut butter cups**
⅓ **cup milk chocolate chips or chopped milk chocolate bar**

1. Beat peanut butter and butter in large bowl with electric mixer at medium speed until well blended. Beat in brown sugar, baking powder and baking soda until blended. Beat in egg and vanilla until well blended. Beat in flour at low speed just until mixed. Stir in peanut butter cups. Cover and refrigerate 1 hour or until firm.

2. Preheat oven to 375°F. For test cookie, measure inside diameter of container. Form ⅓ cup dough into ¼-inch-thick disc, about 2 inches in diameter less than the diameter of container. (One-third cup dough patted into 4-inch disc yields 5-inch cookie. Measure amount of dough used and diameter of cookie before and after baking. Make adjustments before making remaining cookies.)

3. Place dough on ungreased cookie sheets. Bake 10 minutes or until lightly browned. Remove to wire racks; cool completely.

4. Place chocolate chips in small resealable plastic food storage bag; seal bag. Microwave at MEDIUM (50% power) 1 minute. Turn bag over; microwave at MEDIUM 1 minute or until melted. Knead bag until chocolate is smooth. Cut off very tiny corner of bag; pipe chocolate decoratively onto cookies. Let stand until chocolate is set.

5. Stack cookies between layers of waxed paper in container. Store loosely covered at room temperature up to 1 week.

Makes 9 (5-inch) cookies

Spicy Ginger Molasses Cookies

      2 cups all-purpose flour
 1½ teaspoons ground ginger
      1 teaspoon baking soda
   ½ teaspoon ground cloves
   ¼ teaspoon salt
   ¾ cup (1½ sticks) butter, softened
      1 cup sugar
   ¼ cup molasses
      1 egg
         Additional sugar
   ½ cup yogurt-covered raisins

1. Preheat oven to 375°F. Line cookie sheets with parchment paper.

2. Combine flour, ginger, baking soda, cloves and salt in small bowl; set aside.

3. Beat butter and 1 cup sugar in large bowl with electric mixer at medium speed until light and fluffy. Add molasses and egg; beat until well blended. Gradually beat in flour mixture at low speed just until blended.

4. Drop dough by level ¼ cupfuls about 3 inches apart onto prepared cookie sheets; flatten with bottom of glass dipped in additional sugar until cookies are about 2 inches in diameter. Press 8 to 9 yogurt-covered raisins into each cookie.

5. Bake 11 to 12 minutes or until cookies are set. Cool 2 minutes on cookie sheets; slide parchment paper and cookies onto wire racks. Cool completely.

Makes about 1 dozen (4-inch) cookies

A gift from the kitchen of _____

For: _____

A gift from the kitchen of _____

For: _____

A gift from the kitchen of _____

For: _____

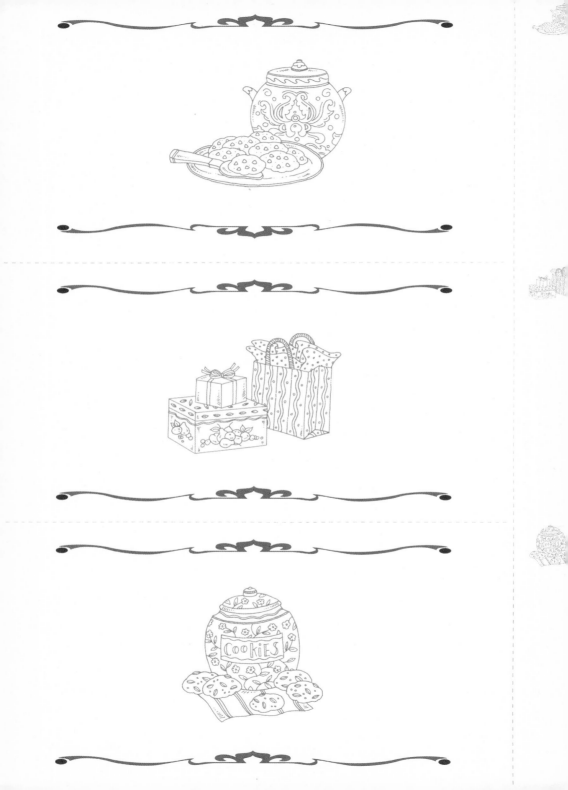

A gift from the kitchen of _____

For: _____

A gift from the kitchen of _____

For: _____

A gift from the kitchen of _____

For: _____

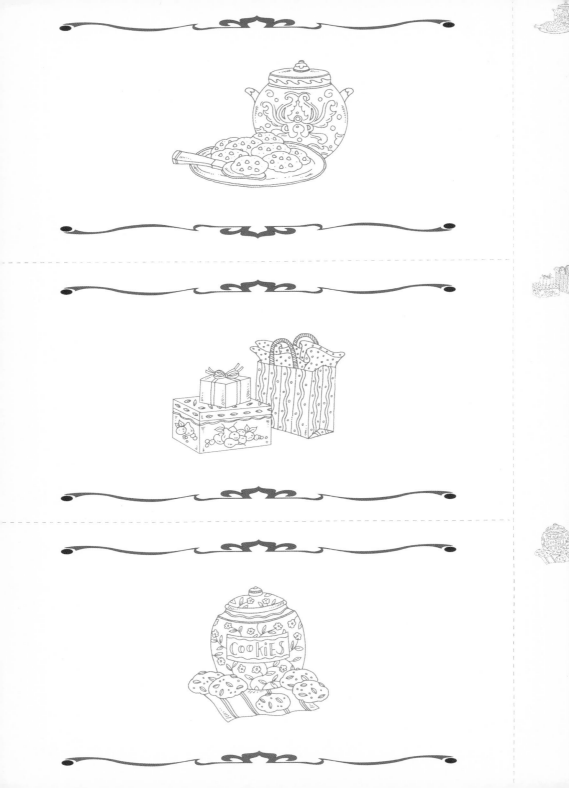

A gift from the kitchen of _____

For: _____

A gift from the kitchen of _____

For: _____

A gift from the kitchen of _____

For: _____

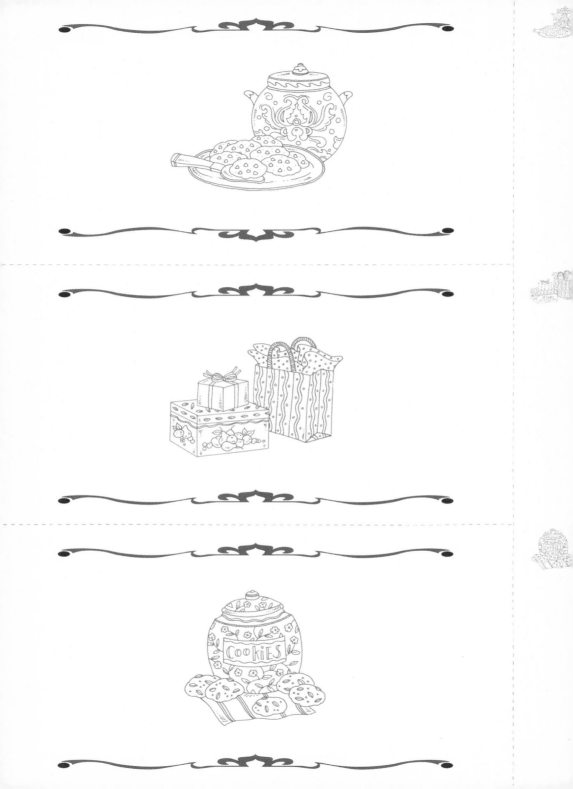

A gift from the kitchen of _____

For: _____

A gift from the kitchen of _____

For: _____

A gift from the kitchen of _____

For: _____

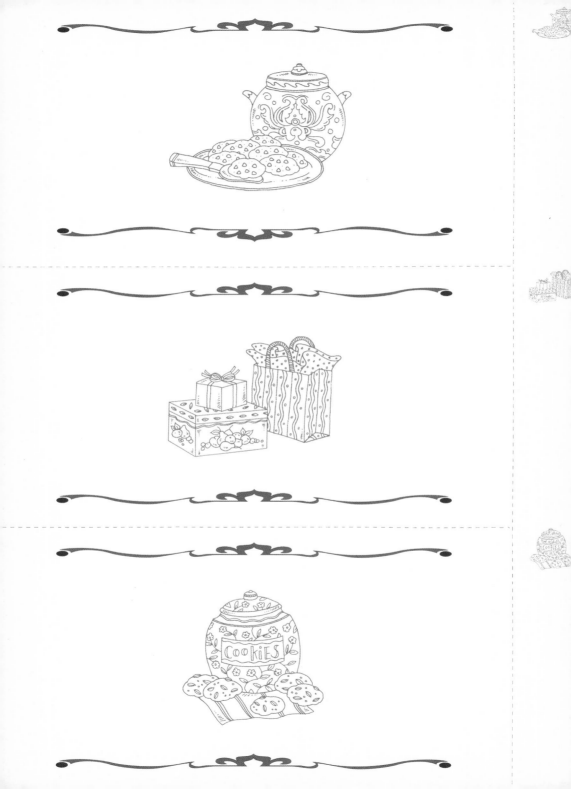

A gift from the kitchen of _____

For: _____

A gift from the kitchen of _____

For: _____

A gift from the kitchen of _____

For: _____

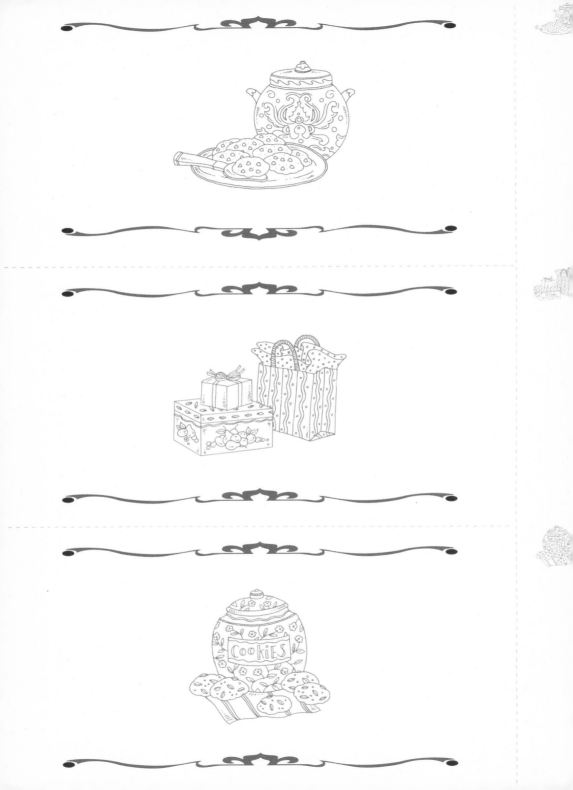

A gift from the kitchen of _____

For: _____

A gift from the kitchen of _____

For: _____

A gift from the kitchen of _____

For: _____

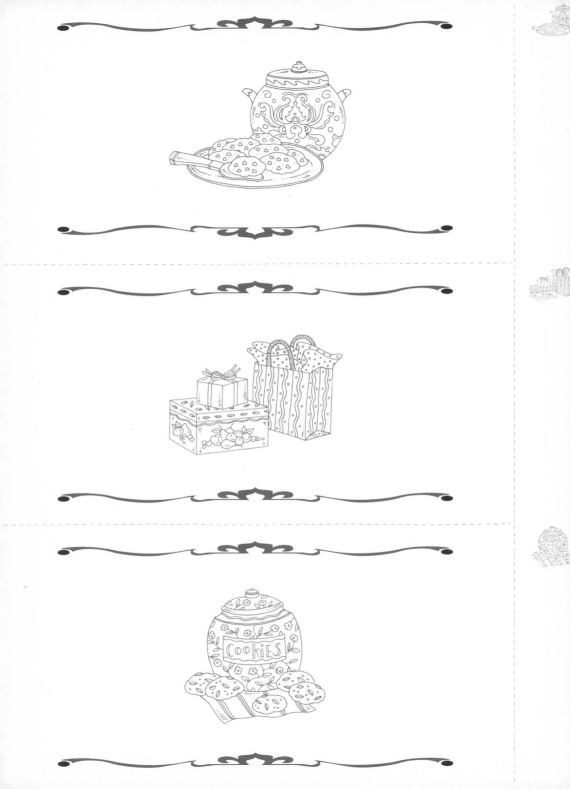

A gift from the kitchen of _____

For: _____

A gift from the kitchen of _____

For: _____

A gift from the kitchen of _____

For: _____

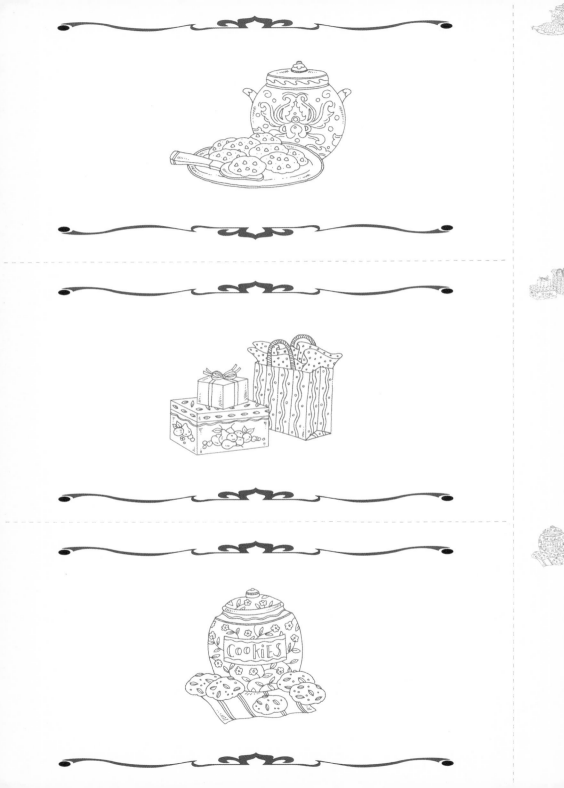

A gift from the kitchen of _____

For: _____

A gift from the kitchen of _____

For: _____

A gift from the kitchen of _____

For: _____

A gift from the kitchen of _____

For: _____

A gift from the kitchen of _____

For: _____

A gift from the kitchen of _____

For: _____

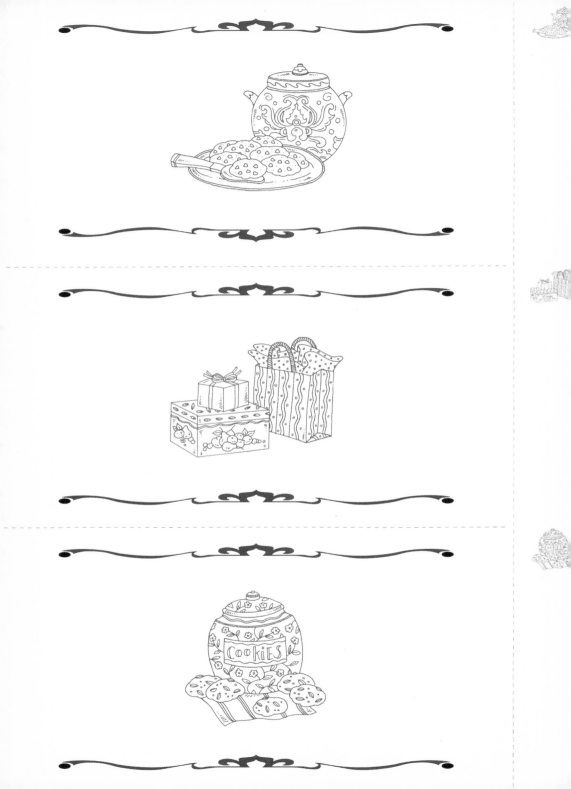

A gift from the kitchen of _____

For: _____

A gift from the kitchen of _____

For: _____

A gift from the kitchen of _____

For: _____

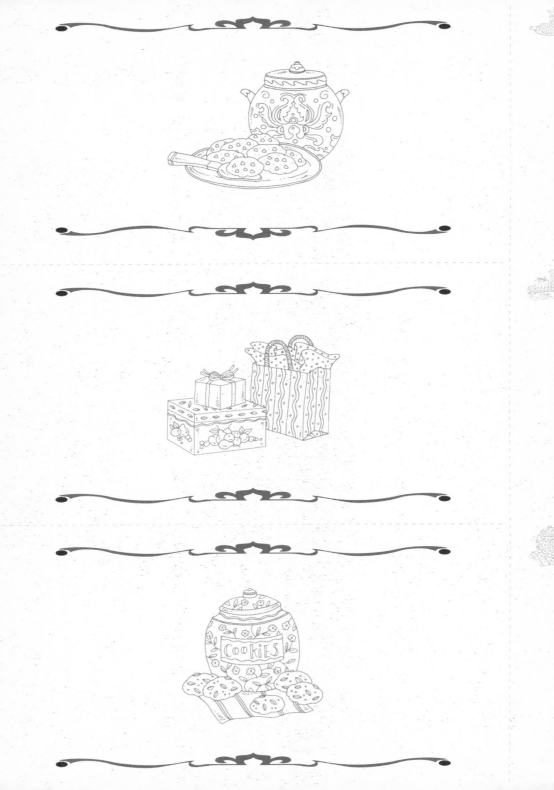

A gift from the kitchen of _____

For: _____

A gift from the kitchen of _____

For: _____

A gift from the kitchen of _____

For: _____

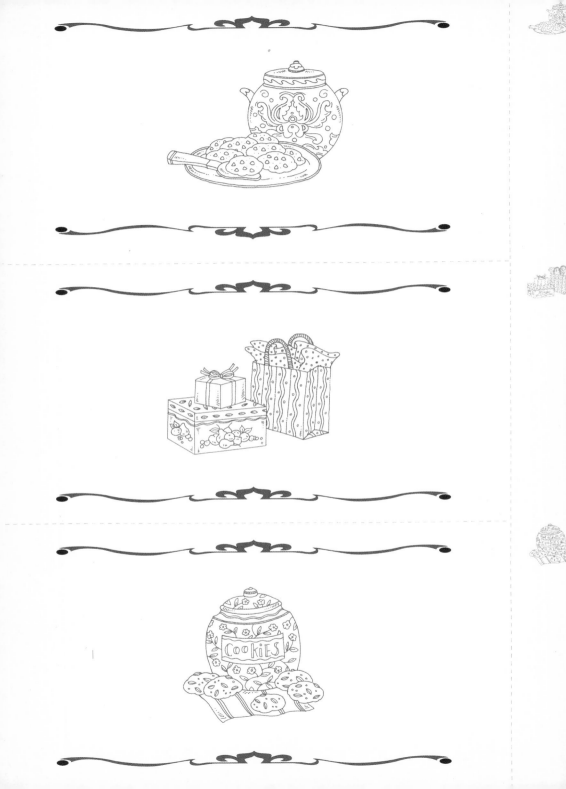

cookies

A gift from the kitchen of _____

For: _____

cookies

A gift from the kitchen of _____

For: _____

cookies

A gift from the kitchen of _____

For: _____

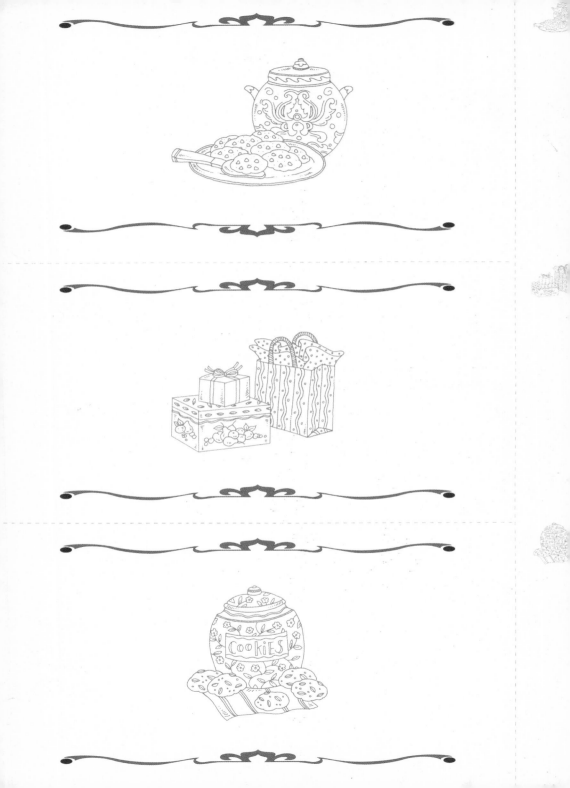